James, 1 & 2 Peter, 1,2,3 John, Rev.

Shalom 2 U, Volume 7

Shalom Jim

Published by SHALOM-JIM, 2023.

JAMES, 1 & 2 PETER, 1,2,3 JOHN, REV.

First edition. February 2, 2023.

ISBN: 979-8215321867

Written by Shalom Jim.

Table of Contents

DEDICATION

To Jesus who sacrificed all so that we would be saved, have eternal life, and become a child of God. He is the bread of life, the Tree of Life, the Light of the World, The Good Shepherd, The Prince of Peace, and the Lamb of God. He is our Redeemer, Savior, Great High Priest, The King of Kings, Deliverer, and Refuge. He is all we need. Glory be to God!

REV. 1:10 INTHESPIRIT
REV 1:16 TWO-EDGEDSWORD
REV 2:2-4 LOVE
REV 2:8-10 BEFAITHFUL
REV 2:12-14 GOOD & BAD
REV 3:1-4 SLEEPINGCHURCH
REV 3:7-10 ENDURE & DON"TDENY
REV 3:18 BUYWITHOUTMONEY

INTRODUCTION

The Gospel is Good News. This book covers the Epistles of James. Peter, John, Jude, and Revelation. The epistles are letters written for the express purpose of telling the Good News. All About Jesus is more than a devotional or bible study. Yes, it is a devotional and a bible study but it also emphasizes Jesus. His name is Jesus: Jehovah Saves. His name implies what He came to do and what He has done for all that have faith in Him. It's' ALL ABOUT JESUS, He actually saves us. Too many ¨ believers¨ believe that He is Our Savior but continually try to save themselves. Our biggest problem is not really knowing and believing, how Jesus does it. God's ways are higher than our ways and His thoughts are higher than our thoughts. Because this book emphasizes Jesus, you will see all of what He has done for us and give Him the honor and praise for it. This is what the Christian Faith is all about. Declaring what He has done for us and then seeing it come to pass in our lives. To God be the glory! Blessings and Shalom 2 u ShalomJim

JAMES 1:2-4 JESUS DELIVERER

Jas 1:2-4 WEB 2 Count it all joy, my brothers, when you fall into various temptations, 3 knowing that the testing of your faith produces endurance. 4 Let endurance have its perfect work, that you may be perfect and complete, lacking in nothing.

Some translations say trials instead of temptations. I think that trials are a better word because it includes everything that we go through in life, including temptations. Whatever trials we are going through, God's word has an answer for it. It's up to us to know, believe, and declare God's promises over that trial. It requires patience and endurance, which are not our best attributes.

Dear Jesus! Thank you for enduring all the trials that you endured while doing the will of the Father. You endured it all for us so that we would overcome the trials that we face. You are not only our Savior but our Deliverer too. Psalm 34:19 NIV The righteous person may have many troubles, but the Lord delivers him from them all; Whatever trial that we are facing today, we cry out to You, our Savior and Deliverer. To God be the glory Amen! Shalom2u

JAMES 1:6-8 DOUBLE-MINDED

Jas 1:6-8 WEB 6 But let him ask in faith, without any doubting, for he who doubts is like a wave of the sea, driven by the wind and tossed. 7 For that man shouldn't think that he will receive anything from the Lord. 8 He is a double-minded man, unstable in all his ways.

I'm sure we all have heard and even said things that were double-minded. It's not easy to be single-minded. We read one of God's promises and our spirit man agrees. Then the flesh will step in and declare the opposite. It seems to be a continual battle. That is why later on in the book of James, he talks about controlling our tongue. God wants us to be like Abraham. Call those things that are not as though they were. Romans 4:17 Darby (according as it is written, I have made thee the father of many nations,) before the God whom he believed, who quickens the dead, and calls the things which be not as being;

Dear Jesus! You are the author and finisher of our faith. Only by abiding in You can we continue to believe and declare Your promises. We shall continually declare that You came to give us life and life more abundantly. To God be the glory Amen! Shalom 2 U

JAMES 1:13-15 TEMPTATIONS

Jas 1:12-15 WEB 12 Blessed is a person who endures temptation, for when he has been approved, he will receive the crown of life, which the Lord promised to those who love him. 13 Let no man say when he is tempted, "I am tempted by God," for God can't be tempted by evil, and he himself tempts no one. 14 But each one is tempted when he is drawn away by his own lust and enticed. 15 Then the lust, when it has conceived, bears sin. The sin, when it is full grown, produces death.

Because of the fall of man, we are born with a sinful nature. Jesus came to save us from that sinful nature. When we are "born again ", we receive a new nature. We become a new creation made in the image and likeness of God. This new creation needs to grow and become mature. Our abiding in Jesus does that. Then we will bear the fruits of the Holy Spirit and die to the lust of the flesh.

Dear Jesus! Your word tells us: 1 John 3:6 DARBY Whoever abides in him, does not sin: whoever sins, has not seen him or known him. Thank you Jesus for setting us free from the lust of this world and giving us Your divine nature of love, peace, joy, and righteousness. To God be the glory Amen! Shalom2u

JAMES 1:18-21 BORN AGAIN

Jas 1:18-21 WEB 18 Of his own will he gave birth to us by the word of truth, that we should be a kind of first fruits of his creatures. 19 So, then, my beloved brothers, let every man be swift to hear, slow to speak, and slow to anger; 20 for the anger of man doesn't produce the righteousness of God. 21 Therefore, putting away all filthiness and overflowing of wickedness, receive with humility the implanted word, which is able to save your souls.

Apostle James tells us that God gave birth to us by the word of Truth. The birth that God gives is a spiritual birth. We are born again into the image and likeness of God by the Word of Truth, Jesus. This is how we are to live and mature. The more we live in the Spirit, we will grow from immature babies to mature children of God. Unfortunately most keep walking in the flesh and fail to mature. That's why so many have a hard time doing what verse 19-20 say. Verse 21 says receive with humility the implanted word that is able to save your soul.

Dear Jesus! You are that seed, the incorruptible word that created us in Your image and likeness. We humbly come to You to grow and mature into Your image and likeness. In You, we are able to put to death the things of the flesh. In You, we walk in the Spirit and produce the fruits of love, peace, joy, etc. To God be the glory Amen! Shalom2u

JAMES 1:23-25 FAITH SPEAKS

Jas 1:23-25 WEB 23 For if anyone is a hearer of the word and not a doer, he is like a man looking at his natural face in a mirror; 24 for he sees himself, and goes away, and immediately forgets what kind of man he was. 25 But he who looks into the perfect law of freedom and continues, not being a hearer who forgets, but a doer of the work, this man will be blessed in what he does.

We are called to live by faith. Jesus did all the work. John 19:30 Darby When therefore Jesus had received the vinegar, he said, It is finished; and having bowed his head, he delivered up his spirit. When we believe and declare what Jesus has done for us, then we are doers of the word. Jesus makes us righteous by faith in Him. 2 Corinthians 5:21 Darby Him who knew not sin he has made sin for us, that we might become God's righteousness in him. Trying to make ourselves righteous only leads to self-righteousness.

Dear Jesus! You came to save us. Your sacrifice did it all. Believing in you is believing in what you have done for us. Thank you for making us righteous, a new creation in your image and likeness, filling us with your peace, love, and joy. We receive all this grace by faith in You. To God be the glory Amen! Shalom2u

JAMES 1:26-27 BRIDLE THE TONGUE

Jas 1:26-27 WEB 26 If anyone among you thinks himself to be religious while he doesn't bridle his tongue, but deceives his heart, this man's religion is worthless. 27 Pure religion and undefiled before our God and Father is this: to visit the fatherless and widows in their affliction, and to keep oneself unstained by the world.

What we say has power. Proverbs 18:21 Darby Death and life are in the power of the tongue, and they that love it shall eat the fruit thereof. Saying who we are in the flesh only keeps us living in the flesh. Saying who we are in Christ Jesus, transforms us into His image and likeness. This is speaking faith words and thereby we are controlling our tongue not to speak unbelief. Then we are empowered to care for the fatherless and widows.

Dear Jesus! You showed love and compassion for all that came to you. You knew that you were in the Father and the Father was in You. We in You and You in us give us the compassion to love and care for one another. To God be the glory Amen! Shalom2u

JAMES 2:21-24 FAITH- WORKS

Jas 2:21-24 WEB 21 Wasn't Abraham our father justified by works, in that he offered up Isaac his son on the altar? 22 You see that faith worked with his works, and by works, faith was perfected. 23 So the Scripture was fulfilled which says, "Abraham believed God, and it was accounted to him as righteousness," and he was called the friend of God. 24 You see then that by works, a man is justified, and not only by faith.

It's hard for me to understand what the Apostle James is saying. Actually, the Bible says that Abraham was justified by faith. Galatians 3:6 Darby. Even as Abraham believed God, and it was reckoned to him as righteousness.

Romans 4:2 web For if Abraham was justified by works, he has something to boast about, but not toward God.

Romans 4:3 DARBY for what does the scripture say? And Abraham believed God, and it was reckoned to him as righteousness. Faith comes before work. The works that truly count are the ones that come from Faith. Jesus is our best example Joh 8:28 WEB Jesus, therefore, said to them, "When you have lifted up the Son of Man, then you will know that I am he, and I do nothing of myself, but as my Father taught me, I say these things. Again in John 6:28 web, They said therefore to him, "What must we do, that we may work the works of God?" Jesus answered them, "This is the work of God, that you believe in him whom he has sent."

The works of God come from faith. It comes from abiding in Jesus. Ephesians 2:10 web For we are his workmanship, created in Christ Jesus for good works, which God prepared before that we would walk in them.

Dear Jesus! You did all that the Father revealed to You to do. Works that no mere human being could do. You said that those who believe in You would do greater works. John 14:12 web Most certainly I tell you, he who believes in me, the works that I do, he will do also; and he will do greater works than these because I am going to my Father.

We shall continually seek You and Your will. You working in us will defeat the darkness and bring light into the world. We command that the blind see, deaf hear, the lame walk, lepers cleansed, and captives set free in Jesus's name Amen! To God be the glory Amen! Shalom2u

JAMES 3:2 OUR WORDS

Jas 3:2 WEB For we all stumble in many things. Anyone who doesn't stumble in word is a perfect person, able to bridle the whole body also.

There are many scriptures that talk about the words we speak. Here are a few.

Psa 39:1 I said, "I will watch my ways, so that I do not sin with my tongue. I will keep my mouth with a bridle while the wicked is before me."

Job 6:24 Teach me, and I will hold my tongue: and cause me to understand wherein I have erred.

Proverbs 18:21 web: Death and life are in the power of the tongue; those who love it will eat its fruit.

Apostle James is telling us of the evil that an untamed tongue can cause. The tongue can cause a lot of good also. When we use the sword of the Spirit, the Word of God, against the kingdom of satan; we are using our tongue correctly. When we use it to bless people, we are using it correctly. When we curse our fellow man; we are using it incorrectly.

Dear Jesus! You went through a lot of trials and suffering from mankind, but you used your tongue correctly. On the cross, you said Father forgive them for they know not what they are doing. Only you living in us, can we have that much patience and understanding for those that hurt us. We pray for your blessings on all mankind. 2 Corinthians 13:14 WEB The grace of the Lord Jesus Christ, God's love, and the fellowship of the Holy Spirit, be with you all. Amen. Shalom 2 U

JAMES 3:10-12 TONGUE: BLESS & CURSE

Jas 3:10-12 WEB 10 Out of the same mouth comes blessing and cursing. My brothers, these things ought not to be so. 11 Does a spring send out from the same opening fresh and bitter water? 12 Can a fig tree, my brothers, yield olives, or vine figs? Thus no spring yields both saltwater and freshwater.

The more that we abide in Jesus, the more we will produce good fruit and speak life-given words to those that need to be blessed. As a priest in the Kingdom of God, we are called to pray for one another. As a King in the Kingdom of God, we take authority over the spirits of darkness.

Dear Jesus! Abiding in You, gives us a heart for the lost and a zeal to fight against the darkness. You are the King of kings and Your name is above all other names. Shalom/ Peace on earth and goodwill to all in Jesus's name Amen. To God be the glory Amen! Shalom2u

1Peter 2:9 web But you are a chosen race, a royal priesthood, a holy nation, a people for God's own possession, that you may proclaim the excellence of him who called you out of darkness into his marvelous light:

JAMES 3:13-15 HEAVENLY WISDOM OR DEMONIC WISDOM

Jas 3:13-15 WEB13 Who is wise and understanding among you? Let him show by his good conduct that his deeds are done in gentleness of wisdom. 14 But if you have bitter jealousy and selfish ambition in your heart, don't boast and don't lie against the truth. 15 This wisdom is not that which comes down from above but is earthly, sensual, and demonic.

So the Apostle James is saying that there are two kinds of wisdom: Godly and demonic. We don't hear the word "demonic " very much in the church or in the world. Yet it is this demonic wisdom and activities that are causing all this darkness in the world. We have too many so-called wise leaders calling good evil and evil good. It wasn't that long ago that some of these leaders were saying just the opposite.

Dear Jesus! It is so easy to be deceived. When we care more about ourselves and less about others and Your Kingdom. You are our wisdom, righteousness, our Good Shepherd that keeps us from being led astray. We only listen to Your voice that gives us life. To God be the glory Amen. Shalom 2u

James 3:17 web But the wisdom that is from above is first pure, then peaceful, gentle, reasonable, full of mercy and good fruits, without partiality, and without hypocrisy.

JAMES 4:3-4 LUST & IDOLATRY

Jas 4:3-4 WEB 3 You ask, and don't receive, because you ask with wrong motives, so that you may spend it on your pleasures. 4 You adulterers and adulteresses, don't you know that friendship with the world is hostility toward God? Whoever therefore wants to be a friend of the world makes himself an enemy of God.

Apostle James seems to be judging, which some say that we shouldn't do. Even Jesus judged the Pharisees.

So James is telling the Jews here that lust and being an adulterer are reasons why we don't get our prayers answered. A lot of times, we are praying for the right reason and according to God's will. The problem can be adultery or Idolatry. When we are unfaithful to God, it's adultery and Idolatry. God wants to bless us but He will not unless we put Him first place in our hearts. Spend some good quality time with God. Praise Him, adore Him, and thank Him for all that He has already done and even the things that haven't come to pass yet.

Dear Jesus! The things of the world do occupy our lives more than they should. Forgive us Jesus for not honoring You above all things. Holy Spirit please help us to praise God above all things. We thank You Jesus for Your sacrifice, Your grace, and the abundant life that You give to us. To God be the glory Amen! Shalom 2u

Mt 6:33 KJV But seek ye first the kingdom of God, and his righteousness, and all these things shall be added unto you.

JAMES 4:6-10 RECEIVE GOD'S GRACE

Jas 4:6-10 WEB 6 But he gives more grace. Therefore it says, "God resists the proud, but gives grace to the humble." 7 Be subject therefore to God. Resist the devil, and he will flee from you. 8 Draw near to God, and he will draw near to you. Cleanse your hands, you sinners. Purify your hearts, you double-minded. 9 Lament, mourn and weep. Let your laughter be turned to mourning, and your joy to gloom. 10 Humble yourselves in the sight of the Lord, and he will exalt you.

We hear that God is gracious. He wants everyone to receive His grace. It says here that grace is given to the humble, not the proud. We humble ourselves when we put God first place in our lives. When we agree with what God says over what man says.

Dear Jesus! Grace is what is needed to be saved. You are the source of all grace. We humbly come to You to receive that grace to save our souls and give us abundant life in You. To God be the glory Amen! Shalom 2u

Mat 5:3 Blessed are the poor in spirit, for theirs is the Kingdom of Heaven.

JAMES 5:14-16 PRAYER OF FAITH

Jas 5:14-16 WEB14 Is any among you sick? Let him call for the elders of the assembly, and let them pray over him, anointing him with oil in the name of the Lord, 15 and the prayer of faith will heal him who is sick, and the Lord will raise him up. If he has committed sins, he will be forgiven. 16 Confess your offenses to one another, and pray for one another, that you may be healed. The insistent prayer of a righteous person is powerfully effective.

Mar 16:17-18 WEB 17 These signs will accompany those who believe: in my name, they will cast out demons; they will speak with new languages; 18 they will take up serpents; and if they drink any deadly thing, it will in no way hurt them; they will lay hands on the sick, and they will recover."

We can see from these scriptures and others, that it is God's will for people to be healed and set free. I realize that it's not an easy task. If it was, you and I would be going around healing everyone that we meet. Nonetheless, it is God's will. Let's never give up. We might not be called individually to heal the sick and cast out demons but we all have a part to play. We need to pray for all our religious leaders, the body of Christ that God's anointing will fall on them as they go and declare God's Good News.

Dear Jesus! We see in Your word what You did for all mankind and Your desire that all be Saved: body, soul, and spirit. You are the head of the body. You are the author and finisher of our faith. We seek Your anointing on all the body of Christ so that Your will be done. 2 Corinthians 13:14 NIV May the grace of the Lord Jesus Christ, and the love of God, and the fellowship of the Holy Spirit be with you all. To God be the glory Amen! Shalom 2u

1 PETER 1:2 SANCTIFIED

1Pe 1:2 WEB according to the foreknowledge of God the Father, in sanctification of the Spirit, that you may obey Jesus Christ and be sprinkled with his blood: Grace to you and peace be multiplied.

Most of us will focus on: that you may obey. If we don't focus on what is first said; we will put ourselves under the law. It says that we are sanctified by the Spirit. Sanctified: holy, pure, righteous, dedicated; these are all received as gifts, Grace by faith in Jesus Christ. That's why it always comes back to know, believe, and declare by faith who you are in Christ Jesus.

Dear Jesus! 1Pe 1:2 WEB according to the foreknowledge of God the Father, in sanctification of the Spirit, that you may obey Jesus Christ and be sprinkled with his blood: Grace to you and peace be multiplied.

Thank you for the gift of Grace. You are the source of Grace. By your Grace, we can love God with all our hearts and souls and our neighbors as ourselves. To God be the glory Amen! Shalom 2u

2Pe 1:2 WEB Grace to you and peace be multiplied in the knowledge of God and of Jesus our Lord,

1 PETER 1:3-7 BORN AGAIN

1Pe 1:3-7 WEB 3 Blessed be the God and Father of our Lord Jesus Christ, who according to his great mercy caused us to be born again to a living hope through the resurrection of Jesus Christ from the dead, 4 to an incorruptible and undefiled inheritance that doesn't fade away, reserved in Heaven for you, 5 who by the power of God are guarded through faith for a salvation ready to be revealed in the last time. 6 Wherein you greatly rejoice, though now for a little while, if need be, you have been grieved in various trials, 7 that the proof of your faith, which is more precious than gold that perishes even though it is tested by fire, may be found to result in praise, glory, and honor at the revelation of Jesus Christ—" **begotten again** ": being **Born Again**. Man was originally created in the image and likeness of God. Because of Adam's disobedience, we lost that image therefore we have to be born again. Once we receive Jesus as our Savior, we are born again. This is what we are called to believe. It says of incorruptible seed. This incorruptible seed needs to grow and as it grows; we become more and more like Jesus. The problem with most Christians is that we continue to focus on the old man. We declare who we are in the flesh and so we don't grow in the Spirit. It doesn't take faith to say who we are in the flesh. It does take faith to declare who we are in the Spirit, the New Man, the New Creation in Christ Jesus.

Dear Jesus! All that we are comes by faith in You. Abiding in You, believing what You have done for us allows that incorruptible seed to grow and bears fruit for Your honor and glory. To God be the glory Amen! Shalom2u

1 Peter 1:8-10 FAITH: BELIEVING BUT NOT SEEING

1Pe 1:8-10 WEB 8 whom, not having known, you love. In him, though now you don't see him, yet believing, you rejoice greatly with joy that is unspeakable and full of glory, 9 receiving the result of your faith, the salvation of your souls. 10 Concerning this salvation, the prophets sought and searched diligently. They prophesied of the grace that would come to you,

We have not seen Jesus, but yet we believe in Him. This is the basis of faith. The more that we believe in Him, the more we will grow in our Christian Faith. When we believe what Jesus has done (not ourselves), we receive grace: God's unmerited favor. This is how God works in us. The result is the salvation of our souls.

Dear Jesus! You are the bread of life. We feed on all that you have done for us. We declare your great and precious promises by which you work in us for the salvation of our souls. To God be the glory Amen! Shalom 2 U

1 Peter 1:13 REVELATION

1Pe 1:13 NHEB Therefore, prepare your minds for action, be sober and set your hope fully on the grace that will be brought to you at the revelation of Jesus Christ.

Apostle Peter is telling us a few things to ponder on! The revelation of Jesus Christ is not something that is going to help us after we die. We need that "revelation " now. It's the revelation of Jesus in our lives that gives us the grace that we need to live righteously. The more we get to know Jesus, the more He is revealed in our lives.

Dear Jesus! There are many seeking grace to live their lives more like You. You are the source of all grace. You are the source of all life. The more we know and believe in You, Jesus, the more we grow in grace. 2Pe 1:2 Grace and peace be multiplied unto you through the knowledge of God, and of Jesus, our Lord, Thank You for giving us life. To God be the glory Amen! Shalom2u

1 Peter 1:18-19 REDEEMED

1Pe 1:18-19 WEB 18 knowing that you were redeemed, not with corruptible things, with silver or gold, from the useless way of life handed down from your fathers, 19 but with precious blood, as of a lamb without blemish or spot, the blood of Christ,

The Bible tells us that we are " redeemed ". We are redeemed because Jesus is our Redeemer. It's important to understand what redeemed means: to release on receipt of ransom,

to redeem, liberate by payment of ransom

to cause to be released to one's self by payment of a ransom

.to redeem: to deliver: from evils of every kind, internal and external

When we believe in Jesus, we are called to believe He is our Redeemer and has redeemed us. Deuteronomy 28 tells us of all the curses of the Law. Believers are called to know and believe that Jesus paid the price through His sacrifice and therefore we are redeemed. We are redeemed when we know, believe, and declare our redemption in Christ Jesus.

Psalms 107:2 NKJV Let the redeemed of the Lord say so, Whom He has redeemed from the hand of the enemy,

Galatians 3:13 WEB Christ redeemed us from the curse of the law, having become a curse for us. For it is written, "Cursed is everyone who hangs on a tree,"

TITUS 2:14 niv who gave himself for us to redeem us from all wickedness and to purify for himself a people that are his very own, eager to do what is good.

Dear Jesus! You have redeemed us by Your sacrifice through Your blood. Redeemed from the curse of the law. Redeemed from the power of Satan. To God be the glory Amen! Shalom2u

1 PETER 1:19 BLOOD OF JESUS

1Pe 1:19 WEB but with precious blood, as of a lamb without blemish or spot, the blood of Christ,

The Bible tells us how God would accept blood sacrifice for the sinner to be forgiven. It couldn't be just any blood sacrifice but a very special sacrifice. One that requires a spotless lamb. That's why Jesus is called the Lamb of God.

Dear Jesus! We thank you and praise you for Your sacrifice. Your sacrifice was total and complete, once and for all. As we abide in You, we are continually wasted clean by Your blood. Your blood also gives us life, for life is in Your blood. May we be a blessing to all as You continue to live in us. To God be the glory Amen! Shalom2u

Son 4:7 KJV Thou art all fair, my love; there is no spot in thee.

1 Peter 1:21 TRANSFORM BY JESUS

1Pe 1:21 WEB who through him are believers in God, who raised him from the dead, and gave him glory, so that your faith and hope might be in God.

It's good to ask ourselves, where is our faith? If we answer, in ourselves; we're going in the wrong direction. Our faith has to be in Jesus. It's what He did for us that counts. Who we are by faith in Him.

Dear Jesus! When we believe all that you did for us; we are in awesome wonder. The Universe that you have created amazes us to no end. What is even more amazing is how you transform us from glory to glory, as we abide in You. To God be the glory Amen! Shalom2u

1 Peter 1:23 INCORRUPTIBLE SEED

1Pe 1:23 WEB having been born again, not of corruptible seed, but of incorruptible, through the word of God, which lives and remains forever.

" Incorruptible seed " cannot be destroyed but it still needs to grow and produce fruit. Meditating on the word brings revelation which helps our faith to produce fruit. Fruit only lasts for a limited time. Fruit has seeds in it so that it can produce more fruit. As we continue to abide in Jesus, the incorruptible seed in us will continue to bear more fruit: love, peace, joy, self control, patience, meekness, etc..

Dear Jesus! You give us abundant life. In you, we are a "New Creation ". You fill us with so much love, peace, and joy that we just want to pass it on to others. Hebrews 13:20□-□21 NKJV Now may the God of peace who brought up our Lord Jesus from the dead, that great Shepherd of the sheep, through the blood of the everlasting covenant, make you complete in every good work to do His will, working in you what is well pleasing in His sight, through Jesus Christ, to whom be glory forever and ever. Amen. Shalom 2 U

1 PETER 2:2 NEED TO GROW

1Pe 2:2 WEB as newborn babies, long for the pure milk of the Word, that with it you may grow,

We need to feed on the word of GOD to grow. Jesus is the Word that became flesh and dwelt among us. When we are first "born again ", we are like babies. Jesus takes special care of us and we need to feed on the pure milk of God's Word. This represents some basic truths of the Gospel. There are fundamental truths like John 3:16. Easy to swallow. Easy to take in. The problem with the church is that we are fed too much milk and not enough meat to fully mature.

Dear Jesus! You have done exceedingly, abundantly more than we can think or imagine. As we continue to abide in You, help us to grow and mature in You. Then we will be able to fight for You Kingdom and come against the power of darkness. To God be the glory Amen! Shalom2u

1 PETER 2:5 HOLY PRIEST

1Pe 2:5 WEB You also, as living stones, are built up as a spiritual house, to be a holy priesthood, to offer up spiritual sacrifices, acceptable to God through Jesus Christ.

JESUS is our High Priest. WE are priests in HIM.

1Pe 2:-9. But you are a chosen race, a royal priesthood, a holy nation, a people for God's own possession, that you may proclaim the excellence of him who called you out of darkness into his marvelous light:

Everyone in the body of Christ is a priest and a king: royal priesthood. There are specially appointed members in the body of Christ that have specific and higher callings but we all are called to act like " spiritual " kings and priests. We all are called as kings to spiritually fight against the spirits of darkness. As priests, we are all called to pray for one another, especially the lost.

Dear Jesus! You left us with authority and a command to preach the Gospel, lay hands on the sick and cast out demons. You are the author and perfecter of our faith. Help us to grow in faith to do Your will here on earth. To God be the glory Amen! Shalom2u

1 PETER 2:6 JESUS: CORNERSTONE

1Pe 2:6 WEB Because it is contained in Scripture, "Behold, I lay in Zion a chief cornerstone, chosen and precious: He who believes in him will not be disappointed."

Everything that we do and believe must be founded on the cornerstone : Jesus. It's not about what we can do or who we are individually. It's about who we are in Christ and what He has done. This is believing in Him.

Dear Jesus! You are the foundation of our faith. It's your sacrifice that makes us children of God. It's Your blood that cleansed us from all unrighteousness. You have done exceedingly, abundantly more than we can ask and imagine. To God be the glory Amen! Shalom2u

1 PETER 2:11 NO LUST IN JESUS

1Pe 2:11 WEB Beloved, I beg you as foreigners and pilgrims, to abstain from fleshly lusts, which war against the soul;

Apostle Peter is telling us two things here. First that we are pilgrims; this is not really our home. To abstain from fleshly lust, we must walk in the spirit. We are pilgrims here but we must identify ourselves with our New Creation spirit. The more we identify who we are in Christ Jesus, the more we will live like Him. This will help us to abstain from fleshly lust.

Dear Jesus! The more that we abide in You, the more we are able to live like You. You give life to our souls which help us to defeat the things of this world. In you we overcome the lust of the flesh. Ephesians, 5:29. For no man ever hated his own flesh; but nourishes and cherishes it, even as the Lord also does the assembly; 30. because we are members of his body, of his flesh and bones. All glory and honor to you Lord Jesus Amen! Shalom 2 U

1 PETER 2:15 HONOR GOD

1Pe 2:15 WEB For this is the will of God, that by well-doing you should put to silence the ignorance of foolish men:

As Christians, we are called to do good works (not to be saved) and live godly so that others can see the love of God in us. There are many good charities and ministries. Why not give and help them that are bringing forth good fruit for the glory of God instead of the glory of mankind.

Dear Jesus! Everything that you did for us, gave glory to the Father. That's why He said this is my beloved Son in whom I am well pleased. As we offer our gifts and lives to You, help us see where You will be glorified in our giving. To God be the glory Amen! Shalom2u

1 PETER 2:24 GOOD NEWS

1Pe 2:24 WEB He himself bore our sins in his body on the tree, that we, having died to sins, might live to righteousness. You were healed by his wounds.

What a beautiful verse. It declares some extremely, overwhelming GOOD NEWS. It's declaring what Jesus has done for us. As Jesus said on the cross: It is finished. He bore our sins so now we don't have to. As long as we look at our flesh instead of our New Creation in Christ Jesus, we will see ourselves as sinners and unrighteous. Only in Christ Jesus can we see ourselves as righteous. Remember, righteousness is a gift received by faith in Jesus. It goes on and declares that by Jesus' wounds, we were healed. Again the flesh we deny it. It is a battle. The spirit wars against the flesh and the flesh against the spirit. It is a very tough battle. It requires faith and patience.

Dear Jesus! You have done exceedingly abundantly above all that we can think or imagine. As we abide in You, helps us to keep our eyes on you and not what we see in the flesh. Be it done according to Your word. To God be the glory Amen! Shalom2u

Mat 8:17 NHEB that it might be fulfilled which was spoken through Isaiah the prophet, saying: "He took our infirmities, and bore our diseases."

1 PETER 2:25 OUR SHEPHERD

1Pe 2:25 WEB For you were going astray like sheep; but now you have returned to the Shepherd and Overseer of your souls.

We are compared to sheep in the Bible. Some are a part of Jesus' flock and some are not. Even those that belong to Jesus, sometimes go astray. We always have a free will, so we don't always stay close to Him.

Dear Jesus! Thank you for taking such good care of us. You feed, protect and guide us. Even when we go astray, you keep searching and calling us back to you. You never give up on us, our family and loved ones. We lie down in green pasture as You look after us. To God be the glory Amen! Shalom2u

1 PETER 3:12 LORD BLESSES

1Pe 3:9-10 WEB9 not rendering evil for evil, or insult for insult; but instead blessing, knowing that you were called to this, that you may inherit a blessing. 10 For, "He who would love life and see good days, let him keep his tongue from evil and his lips from speaking deceit.

1Pe 3:12 WEB For the eyes of the Lord are on the righteous, and his ears open to their prayer; but the face of the Lord is against those who do evil."

This chapter starts off with how wives show reverence to their husband and husband to love their wives. We all know that it can be very challenging at times, especially when one is going in the wrong direction. My wife and I have been married now for over 57 years. We both have had our own faults and ups and downs. Our faith in the Lord has helped us along the way. I believe that it would have been much more fruitful and easier if we took the Lord's advice sooner.

Dear Jesus! You gave us such a great example of how to love. You didn't condemn but was patient, loving and kind. You laid down your life. You humble yourself so that others would see the love of the Father. Even now You are our High Priest making intercession for us now. May we continue to abide in You and Your grace and love one another. To God be the glory Amen! Shalom 2 U

1 PETER 3:18 THE FLESH IS DEAD

1Pe 3:18 WEB Because Christ also suffered for sins once, the righteous for the unrighteous, that he might bring you to God, being put to death in the flesh, but made alive in the Spirit,

What is God trying to tell us here; " The flesh is dead ". We know that we can still feel pain, pleasure, hunger in the flesh. How can our flesh be dead? God is telling us here that we are now a New Creation in Christ Jesus. We are to declare who we are now that Jesus has saved us. This is how we " walk in the Spirit ". Declaring who we are in the flesh, only keeps the flesh alive to do the deeds of the flesh. Declaring who we are in the spirit, allows the Holy Spirit to work in us. This is how we are transformed from living according to the flesh, to live according to the Spirit.

Dear Jesus! You said before you left this world, that the Holy Spirit would come and be our helper. The saying " the flesh is willing but the spirit is weak " doesn't apply to us now. Now we have the power of the Holy Spirit and Your word to put to death the deeds of the flesh and live unto righteousness. To God be the glory Amen! Shalom2u

Rom 8:10 If Christ is in you, the body is dead because of sin, but the spirit is alive because of righteousness.

1 PETER 4:1-3 DIE TO SELF

1Pe 4:1-3 WEB 1 Therefore, since Christ suffered for us in the flesh, arm yourselves also with the same mind; for he who has suffered in the flesh has ceased from sin, 2 that you no longer should live the rest of your time in the flesh for the lusts of men, but for the will of God. 3 For we have spent enough of our past time doing the desire of the Gentiles, and having walked in lewdness, lusts, drunken binges, orgies, carousings, and abominable idolatries.

We know how much Jesus suffered in the flesh for us. Because of His great sacrifice, we should stop doing unrighteous things in the flesh. We all are tempted and easily fail, when we try to do it on our own. When we deny our flesh and spend time with the Lord; then we find the strength to resist the temptation in life. We receive Grace from Jesus that transforms us into His image and likeness. This is how we "walk in the Spirit" and not in the flesh.

Dear Jesus! You are always faithful, when we come to You. In You, we are more than conquerors. In You, we can defeat the lust of the flesh. You bring us out of our darkness into Your marvelous light. To God be the glory Amen! Shalom2u

1 PETER 4:6 LIVE IN THE SPIRIT

1Pe 4:6 WEB For to this end the Good News was preached even to the dead, that they might be judged indeed as men in the flesh, but live as to God in the spirit.

The New Testament tells us to " walk in the Spirit " and not in the flesh. The Holy Spirit is telling us here that if we walk in the Spirit we are alive to God. Walking in your New Creation Spirit is walking in the Spirit. You no longer identify who you are in the flesh. That's how you put to death the flesh. You are a New Creation in the image and likeness of God. You are holy, righteousness, wise, full of love, peace, joy, mercy, temperance, compassion, patience in the Holy Spirit. As we praise God for making us like Him, we will be transformed into His image.

Dear Jesus! We thank you, for only You could make us alive again: " born again " . To identify who we are in the flesh only deny's who we are in You. It's like saying that you did nothing to save us. We stand with Job and declare: And as for me, I know that my Redeemer liveth, and the Last, he shall stand upon the earth; Job 19:25 DARBY

You are the one who puts the deeds of the flesh to death as we proclaim our identity in You. To God be the glory Amen! Shalom2u

1 PETER 4:8 LOVE COVERS

1Pe 4:8 WEB And above all things be earnest in your love among yourselves, for love covers a multitude of sins.

When I read this verse, I am reminded of two people. I have a close relative that one could say was the black sheep in the family. Nonetheless, he loves his family, close relatives, and friends. I would remind the Lord that His Word says, love covers a multitude of sins. The Lord has been faithful in doing that.

Dear Jesus! Love covers a multitude of sins. Your love has done that for us. No matter how much and how far we strayed away from you. When we come back to you ; your love not only covers our sins but wash them away. To God be the glory Amen! Shalom2u

1 PETER 4:13-16 SUFFERING

1Pe 4:13-16 WEB 13 But because you are partakers of Christ's sufferings, rejoice, that at the revelation of his glory you also may rejoice with exceeding joy. 14 If you are insulted for the name of Christ, you are blessed; because the Spirit of glory and of God rests on you. On their part he is blasphemed, but on your part he is glorified. 15 For let none of you suffer as a murderer, or a thief, or an evil doer, or a meddler in other men's matters. 16 But if one of you suffers for being a Christian, let him not be ashamed; but let him glorify God in this matter.

First we need to establish that the suffering talked about here is not the suffering from some sickness or disease. Jesus never suffered from sickness or disease! This suffering is a result of being a Christian. It's most evident in foreign countries where they don't allow religion like China or believe in a different type of religion like the middle eastern countries. We suffer somewhat here in America. We will be called names, be forbidden to speak, and lack opportunities to advance in some careers. Whatever we suffer, we rejoice and give glory to God.

Dear Jesus! You rejoiced in the suffering that you endured because you knew that it would lead to our salvation. We rejoice in our suffering that glorifies you and leads many to come to You. To God be the glory Amen! Shalom2u

1 PETER 5:7 CASTING OUR CARES

1Pe 5:7 KJV Casting all your care upon him; for he careth for you.

The world is full of things to fear and be worried about. John 16:33 kjv these things I have spoken unto you, that in me ye might have peace. in the world ye shall have tribulation: but be of good cheer; I have overcome the world..

Jesus knows all the problems that we have to deal with but he says " be of good cheer ". I wonder how many ;" you must be crazy looks" Jesus got after saying those words. He might not have gotten any. By this time, the apostles were with Jesus a long time. This is what we need to do; spend time in Jesus' presents. meditate on his words, to you. talk to him and give him praise. Then your faith will grow to believe.

Dear Jesus ! Thank you for caring for me so much that by your suffering , I can receive your peace. You are Jehovah Shalom. You take my cares away and give me your peace. Glory be to God. amen ! SHALOM2U

1 PETER 5:8 YOUR ADVERSARY

1Pe 5:8 WEB Be sober and self-controlled. Be watchful. Your adversary, the devil, walks around like a roaring lion, seeking whom he may devour.

It appears from this verse that there are those that the devil can harm & there are those that the devil can not harm. Why? Maybe because one is not fighting the good fight of faith. see v9. Also: Hos 4:6 KJV My people are destroyed for lack of knowledge: because thou hast rejected knowledge, I will also reject thee, that thou shalt be no priest to me: seeing thou hast forgotten the law of thy God, I will also forget thy children.

Believing what others say instead of what God says. One must meditate on the Word themselves. Remember we are not under the Law but Grace. Grace will enable one to fulfill the Law and more. We must believe that we are more than conquerors, that we have authority, that we are redeemed from the curse of the law and have the blessing of Abraham. I, like many others, used to believe that bad things happen and it's a part of life. God's word tells us differently.

Dear Jesus! You told us that you came to give us life and life more abundantly. Your Word tells us that we are more than conquerors and redeemed from the curse of the law. The flesh keeps on telling us differently. As the author and perfecter of our faith, we look to you. Help us to believe that with God, nothing is impossible. To God be the glory Amen. Shalom2u

2 PETER 1:2 GRACE & PEACE

2Pe 1:2 WEB Grace to you and peace be multiplied in the knowledge of God and of Jesus our Lord,

We all seek Grace & Peace. God's will for us is to receive His grace & peace. The problem is we seek it, the wrong way. We rely on others to receive these things.

This verse tells us that it's all about knowing God and Jesus our Saviour. Grace comes from Christ Jesus. It's freely given to all who believe. Knowing, believing, and declaring who Jesus is to you.

Dear Jesus! You are the source of life. You are the source of all grace. You are the one who makes us righteous. Thank you for changing us into Your image and likeness. To God be the glory Amen! Shalom 2u

Col 1:10 KJV That ye might walk worthy of the Lord unto all pleasing, being fruitful in every good work, and increasing in the knowledge of God;

2 PETER 1:3-4 DIVINE POWER

2Pe 1:3-4 WEB3 seeing that his divine power has granted to us all things that pertain to life and godliness, through the knowledge of him who called us by his own glory and virtue, 4 by which he has granted to us his precious and exceedingly great promises; that through these you may become partakers of the divine nature, having escaped from the corruption that is in the world by lust.

HIS Divine power: GOD's Word, GOD' s Holy Spirit, GOD' s Son-Jesus Christ , the name of Jesus.

We all come to believe that God has infinite power, Divine power. What we fail to believe is that " in Christ Jesus " , Divine power has been given to us. We act like humans instead of children of God. Verse 4 says that we are to be partakers of the Divine nature.

Dear Jesus! It's all about You and it's all about who we are in You. You have given us Your Divine nature but we keep looking at our human nature. Those exceedingly great precious promises are hard to believe and receive. Only spending time in Your and the Holy Spirit's presence can help us to believe. To God be the glory Amen! Shalom 2u

Psa 8:6 KJV Thou madest him to have dominion over the works of thy hands; thou hast put all things under his feet:

2 PETER 1:8-9 KNOW JESUS

2Pe 1:8-9 WEB8 For if these things are yours and abound, they make you to not be idle or unfruitful in the knowledge of our Lord Jesus Christ. 9 For he who lacks these things is blind, seeing only what is near, having forgotten the cleansing from his old sins.

The Holy Spirit talks about living a godly life and then says that we will be fruitful in the knowledge of Jesus Christ. He reminds us that we were cleansed from old sins. What about new sins? Just as we were cleansed from old sins by faith in Jesus not our own works. As we abide in Jesus, He will cleanse us again.

Dear Jesus! We thank you for never giving up on us. Your Word tells us that

Proverbs 24:16 WEB for a righteous man falls seven times, and rises up again; but the wicked are overthrown by calamity.

It's You that picks us up again and again. To God be the glory Amen! Shalom 2u

2 PETER 2:1 FALSE PROPHETS

2Pe 2:1 WEB But false prophets also arose among the people, as false teachers will also be among you, who will secretly bring in destructive heresies, denying even the Master who bought them, bringing on themselves swift destruction.

Apostle Peter is talking about false prophets and teachers in his day and days to follow. I am amazed how quickly the Gospel can be misinterpreted. It started out as Good News and all about Grace from faith in Jesus Christ. The book of Galatians goes into it. There is no other Gospel but the Gospel of Grace. For many years following Peter 's warning the Gospel of Grace was replaced with the gospel of law and works. It's only been 500 years ago that the Gospel of saved by grace through faith was preached. Martin Luther was persecuted by the church for trying to get the Gospel out to all people. Isn't that what Jesus wanted the church to do?

Dear Jesus! We thank you for your Gospel, the Gospel of Grace . We thank You for raising up preachers and teachers that declare the Gospel of Grace. As we abide in You, You give us the Grace that changes us from the inside out. It's not our work but only your Grace. To God be the glory Amen! Shalom 2u

2 PETER 2:7-9 RIGHTEOUS LOT

2Pe 2:7-9 WEB 7 and delivered righteous Lot, who was very distressed by the lustful life of the wicked 8 (for that righteous man dwelling among them was tormented in his righteous soul from day to day with seeing and hearing lawless deeds): 9 the Lord knows how to deliver the godly out of temptation and to keep the unrighteous under punishment for the day of judgment,

It puzzles me how Lot was considered "just ". But we're considered " just, righteous " not by works but by faith in Jesus Christ. Like Lot, we live among the ungodly. Sometimes their influence rubs on us. It's only by grace, just like Lot, that we are delivered from the ungodly.

Dear Jesus! We do get tormented and enticed by the ungodly. They seem at times like they are enjoying life. Thanks to You, we came to experience life as it is meant to be. You fulfilled our lives with Your love, peace, and joy. We pray for those that haven't yet experienced, Your life. 2 Corinthians 13:14 WEB The grace of the Lord Jesus Christ, God's love, and the fellowship of the Holy Spirit, be with you all. Amen. Shalom 2u

2 PETER 3:3 MOCKERS

2Peter 3:3 WEB knowing this first, that in the last days mockers will come, walking after their own lusts

Again we are being warned that mockers- false prophets will come. They will deny that sin is sinful and claim that their lust is not sinful but love.

Dear Jesus! We thank you for giving us eyes to see that our sins are wrong. That You can circumcise our hearts to love Your word, to love You and others with the love that You have given us. We pray for those that still haven't been set free. In Jesus name: We command the blind to see, deaf to hear, lame walk, lepers cleansed and captives set free. The grace of the Lord Jesus Christ, God's love, and the fellowship of the Holy Spirit, be with you all. Amen! Shalom 2 U

2 PETER 3:18 KNOW JESUS

2Pe 3:18 WEB But grow in the grace and knowledge of our Lord and Savior Jesus Christ. To him be the glory both now and forever. Amen.

As I said before, when we are first born again, we are baby Christians. We need to grow and mature. We don't grow by looking at ourselves. We grow by knowing Jesus. The more we are committed to knowing Jesus, the more we will grow in faith and grace. Spending time in His Word, praising and worshiping Him.

Dear Jesus! You are the author and perfecter of our faith. You are the bread of life. We grow because of You. We grow abiding in You. Thank you for Your grace that helps us live more like You. To God be the glory Amen! Shalom 2u

1 JOHN 1:1-3 TESTIFYING

1Jn 1:1-3 WEB1 That which was from the beginning, that which we have heard, that which we have seen with our eyes, that which we saw, and our hands touched, concerning the Word of life 2 (and the life was revealed, and we have seen, and testify, and declare to you the life, the eternal life, which was with the Father, and was revealed to us); 3 that which we have seen and heard we declare to you, that you also may have fellowship with us. Yes, and our fellowship is with the Father, and with his Son, Jesus Christ.

The Apostle John is writing to believers and non-believers. He is Testifying of his personal relationship with Jesus. This is what we need to experience and declare to others. It seems that the more we make it personal, the more we are likely to receive and believe.

Dear Jesus! You are the one that has given us the fullness of life. Every day, every moment that we focus on you, brings life to our souls. When things aren't going well, when we are under attack, Your peace in us is a testimony to others of You living in us. You are worthy of all praise and thanksgiving. To God be the glory Amen! Shalom 2u

1 JOHN 1:7-9 LIGHT EXPELS DARKNESS

1 Jn 1:7-9 WEB 7 But if we walk in the light, as he is in the light, we have fellowship with one another, and the blood of Jesus Christ, his Son, cleanses us from all sin. 8 If we say that we have no sin, we deceive ourselves, and the truth is not in us. 9 If we confess our sins, he is faithful and righteous to forgive us the sins, and to cleanse us from all unrighteousness.

Too often we try to expel the darkness, the sin in our lives. The world needs to know the Good News. It doesn't say here for us to expel the darkness, the sin in our lives. It says walk in the light. As we fellowship with Jesus, He will expel our darkness.

Dear Jesus! You are the Light of the world. It's Your presence in our lives that expelled the darkness. It's Your blood that cleansed us from all our sins. There is too much darkness in this world. You have all power and authority so in the name of Jesus: " LIGHT BE ". To God be the glory Amen! Shalom 2u

1 Th 5:5 WEB You are all children of light and children of the day. We don't belong to the night, nor to darkness,

1 JOHN 2:1-3 JESUS OUR COUNSELOR

1Jn 2:1-3 WEB1 My little children, I write these things to you so that you may not sin. If anyone sins, we have a Counselor with the Father, Jesus Christ, the righteous. 2 And he is the atoning sacrifice for our sins, and not for ours only, but also for the whole world. 3 This is how we know that we know him: if we keep his commandments.

Strong's Definition: An intercessor, consoler: - advocate, comforter.

summoned, called to one's side, especially called to one's aid

one who pleads another's cause before a judge, a pleader, counsel for defense, legal assistant, an advocate

one who pleads another's cause with one, an intercessor

of Christ in his exaltation at God's right hand, pleading with God the Father for the pardon of our sins

in the widest sense, a helper, succourer, aider, assistant

of the Holy Spirit destined to take the place of Christ with the apostles (after his ascension to the Father), to lead them to a deeper knowledge of the gospel truth, and give them divine strength needed to enable them to undergo trials and persecutions on behalf of the divine kingdom

Above is a list of the meanings of Counselor. As we abide in Jesus, He gives us the Grace not to sin. But if we do sin, Jesus: our Intercessor, intercedes for us. The more we love Jesus and our fellow man, the less we will sin.

Dear Jesus! You always had the love of the Father and the love of mankind in Your heart. Your love in us brings our life and purpose to a higher level. To God be the glory Amen! Shalom 2u

1 JOHN 2:12-14 CHILDREN OF GOD

1Jn 2:12-14 WEB 12 I write to you, little children, because your sins are forgiven you for his name's sake. 13 I write to you, fathers, because you know him who is from the beginning. I write to you, young men, because you have overcome the evil one. I write to you, little children, because you know the Father. 14 I have written to you, fathers, because you know him who is from the beginning. I have written to you, young men, because you are strong, and the word of God remains in you, and you have overcome the evil one.

Children: immature in the faith.

We all are children of God but we are called to grow in Christ. Little children are like babies. They need special care and food that is easy to digest. I see this as a major problem in the church. We keep getting fed milk and very little meat. The next stage of growth is young men. Here they are feeding on meat. Meat in the Bible refers to the hidden meaning of scripture that is only revealed by Meditating on the word. Here again is a big problem in the body of Christ. We aren't taught to meditate. I read the Bible for 30 years and did very little Meditation on it. Thus I was still a little child in the faith. The next phase of Christian growth is to become Father's. Male and female believers that have grown from young Christian to fully mature Christian. This is one that has been through many battles but came through them by fighting the good fight of faith : knowing, believing, and declaring God's great and precious promises in Christ Jesus.

Dear Jesus! We are who we are, only by abiding in You. You are the author of our faith. In You we live. In You we are more than conquerors. All praise, honor, and glory to You, Lord Jesus Amen! Shalom 2u

1 JOHN: 2:15-16 GOD'S LOVE

1Jn 2:15-16 WEB15 Don't love the world or the things that are in the world. If anyone loves the world, the Father's love isn't in him. 16 For all that is in the world, the lust of the flesh, the lust of the eyes, and the pride of life, isn't the Father's, but is the world's.

1ST. Love : an earthly love, basic not heavenly, lust full.

2nd. Love: GOD'S type of love. Unselfish, heavenly

The first love is a selfish, lustful type of love, very narrow and basic. We are called to not lust after things but first seek the Kingdom of God and all these things shall be added unto you. God wants us to have good things but He must come first.

Dear Jesus! You gave up all the things that one can desire. You were up there in Your Kingdom enjoying everything. Yet for us, You left it all for us. You really showed us what love and not lust is all about. In You we can love with the love of God. To God be the glory Amen! Shalom 2u

1 JOHN 2:27 ANOINTED

1Jn 2:27 WEB As for you, the anointing which you received from him remains in you, and you don't need anyone to teach you. But as his anointing teaches you concerning all things, and is true, and is no lie, and even as it taught you, you will remain in him.

2Co 1:21 KJV Now he which established us with you in Christ, and hath anointed us, is God;

Every Christian is anointed. Christ means Anointed One. Christians must believe that they are " in Christ ". The more we believe and abide in Him, the more we will live like Him. We can't go by sight or feelings, only by faith.

It says here that you don't need anyone to teach you . Some will take this verse and ignore other verses. We need to know what else the New Testament says like:

1 Corinthians 12:28 WEB God has set some in the assembly: first apostles, second prophets, third teachers, then miracle workers, then gifts of healings, helps, governments, and various kinds of languages. There has to be balance here. If we rely only on what we hear teachers say, we can be led into false teaching. If we only go by what we believe that the Holy Spirit is teaching us, we can believe falsely. I have found that if I get a teaching from the Holy Spirit, I will get confirmation from a minister of God. We don't always agree, so I keep looking. Usually I will hear someone saying the same thing and I will have an inner witness that it is true.

Dear Jesus! You keep on telling us to abide in You. John 15:7 WEB If you remain in me, and my words remain in you, you will ask whatever you desire, and it will be done for you. You are our ultimate teacher and will lead us into all truth as we abide in You. To God be the glory Amen! Shalom 2u

1 JOHN 3:9-10 BORN OF GOD

1Jn 3:9-10 WEB9 Whoever is born of God doesn't commit sin, because his seed remains in him, and he can't sin, because he is born of God. 10 In this the children of God are revealed, and the children of the devil. Whoever doesn't do righteousness is not of God, neither is he who doesn't love his brother.

" Born of God " , " Born Again " , " a New Creation " , these are terms that we must know, believe, and declare. We are called to live by faith and not by sight. This is a big problem in the church. We keep on identifying ourselves in the flesh, instead of the spirit man, the Born again, New Creation man. The Born Again man does not and can not sin. As we give praise and thanksgiving to God for making us His children, we will be transformed and not go on sinning.

Dear Jesus! Thank you for making us a child of God. We now have Your gift of righteousness in us. We are now created in Your image and likeness so that as we believe, we will live more like You. To God be the glory Amen! Shalom 2u

Father by GOD : born again

We become "born again " when we confess that we are a sinner and ask jesus to come into our hearts to save us.

1 JOHN 3:12 REVERENCE GOD'S WORD

1Jn 3:12 WEB unlike Cain, who was of the evil one, and killed his brother. Why did he kill him? Because his deeds were evil, and his brother's righteous.

You see here the difference between two twin brothers. One is declared evil while the other righteous. One didn't have reverence for God's word while the other did. When we just casually read God's word, we are not really showing God how much it means to us. We get it in our minds but not into our souls. It has to be in our souls to bring forth the fruit of righteousness.

Dear Jesus! You said that if we would abide in You, we would bear much fruit. Thank You for doing what we couldn't do on our own. You give us life and life more abundantly. To God be the glory Amen! Shalom 2u

1 JOHN 3:23 NEW COMMANDED: LOVE

1Jn 3:23 WEB This is his commandment, that we should believe in the name of his Son, Jesus Christ, and love one another, even as he commanded.

John 13:34 A new commandment I give to you, that you love one another. Just as I have loved you, you also must love one another. V35 By this everyone will know that you are my disciples, if you have love for one another.``

We see here that John is saying the same thing that Jesus said. John first declares that we believe in Jesus. Some people are naturally loving people but that isn't all that is needed to be saved. Believing in Jesus, really getting to know Him. This causes us to receive His love and be able to love God and love one another.

Dear Jesus! There is no greater love than Your love for us. Even while we were sinners- unrighteous, You the righteous one died for us. Thank you Jesus! To God be the glory Amen! Shalom 2u

1 JOHN 4:4,9,17 LIKE JESUS

1Jn 4:4 WEB You are of God, little children, and have overcome them; because greater is he who is in you than he who is in the world.

1Jn 4:9 WEB By this God's love was revealed in us, that God has sent his only born Son into the world that we might live through him.

1Jn 4:17 WEB In this, love has been made perfect among us, that we may have boldness in the day of judgment, because as he is, even so we are in this world.

When we put all 3 verses together, we get more revelation of what the Holy Spirit is saying. We are called " overcomers" ; not by our own strength but because Jesus lives in us. We get everything we need: wisdom, peace, joy, righteousness, self control, love etc by declaring Jesus living in us.

Dear Jesus! Thank you for making us a New Creation; made in Your image and likeness. You living through us, doing exceedingly abundantly above all that we can think or imagine. To God be the glory Amen! Shalom 2u

Here are some more verses to meditate on.

1Co 1:30 NHEB And because of him you are in Christ Jesus, who became for us wisdom from God, and righteousness and sanctification and redemption,

Eph 5:30 KJV For we are members of his body, of his flesh, and of his bones.

1Co 6:15 KJV Know ye not that your bodies are the members of Christ? shall I then take the members of Christ, and make them the members of an harlot? God forbid.

2Co 3:18 KJV But we all, with open face beholding as in a glass the glory of the Lord, are changed into the same image from glory to glory, even as by the Spirit of the Lord.

2Co 1:21 KJV Now he which established us with you in Christ, and hath anointed us, is God;

1 JOHN 4:9 LIVE THROUGH JESUS

1Jn 4:9 WEB By this God's love was revealed in us, that God has sent his only born Son into the world that we might live **through him**.

Phm 1:6 NHEB that the fellowship of your faith may become effective, in the knowledge of every good thing which is **in us in Christ.**

Phi 2:13 KJV For it is God which **worketh in you** both to will and to do of his good pleasure.

Gal 2:20 NHEB I have been crucified with Christ, and it is **no longer I that live,** but **Christ living in me.** That life which I now live in the flesh, I live by faith in the Son of God, who loved me, and gave himself up for me.

Eph 2:10 WEB For we are **his workmanship**, created **in Christ** Jesus for good works, which God prepared before that we would walk in them.

That we might **live through him**

For over 60 years, I believed in Jesus but tried living the Christian life on my own. These 5 verses tell us that believing in Jesus, is declaring Him working in us, through us. This is what walking in the Spirit is all about.

Dear Jesus! We acknowledge You working in us as we abide in You. You take our human nature and transform it into Your Divine Nature. You work in our lives and do exceedingly, abundantly more than we can ever imagine. We pray that You continue to work in us for Your honor and glory. To God be the glory Amen! Shalom 2u

1 JOHN 4:18 FEARLESS

1Jn 4:18 WEB There is no fear in love; but perfect love casts out fear, because fear has punishment. He who fears is not made perfect in love.

The only thing that we should fear is rejecting God's gift of eternal life. Rejecting Jesus is claiming that one doesn't need to be saved. This is only self righteousness. One will fear when they come to God on their own righteousness.

Dear Jesus! We thank you for all that you have given us, when we received : Your salvation, Your righteousness, Your love. Now we have no fear but only the blessed hope of eternal life with You. To God be the glory Amen! Shalom 2u

1 JOHN 5:1-3 BORN AGAIN

1Jn 5:1-3 WEB 1 Whoever believes that Jesus is the Christ has been born of God. Whoever loves the Father also loves the child who is born of him. 2 By this we know that we love the children of God, when we love God and keep his commandments. 3 For this is loving God, that we keep his commandments. His commandments are not grievous.

It starts off here declaring that we are "Born Again " by faith in Jesus Christ. One can not go by the flesh: outward appearances. It's in the inside of every believer. The problem is that we fail to mature in the Spirit. Meditating on the Word of God, will help one mature in the Spirit. This New Creation spirit is full of God's love As we grow in the Spirit, we will grow in love. Now the commandment of God is love. His commandments are not grievous when we are filled with the love of God.

Dear Jesus! In Your presence is the fullness of love, peace, and joy. Your love in us, makes us love You and others more. Your love makes it easy not grievous to love. To God be the glory Amen! Shalom 2u

1Jn 3:23 KJV And this is his commandment, That we should believe on the name of his Son Jesus Christ, and love one another, as he gave us commandment.

1 JOHN 5:13 FAITH IN JESUS

1Jn 5:13 WEB These things I have written to you who believe in the name of the Son of God, that you may know that you have eternal life, and that you may continue to believe in the name of the Son of God.

We are called to believe in the name of Jesus. It's more than just believing that His name is Jesus. It's about believing all that His name represents. Jesus:

Joshua or Jehoshua = " Jehovah is salvation"

In Hebrew Jesus name represents Jehovah is salvation, Jehovah saves. We are called to believe that Jesus saves us and not ourselves. He saves totally: body, soul, and spirit. The word " salvation " and "save" in Hebrew is " sozo". to save, keep safe and sound, to rescue from danger or destruction, one (from injury or peril), to save a suffering one (from perishing), i.e. one suffering from disease, to make well, heal, restore to health, to preserve one who is in danger of destruction, to save or rescue, to save in the technical biblical sense, negatively : to deliver from the penalties of the Messianic judgment

Jesus saves us completely and that is what we are called to believe. First He makes us " Born Again " which saves us from eternal domination because we must be " Born Again ". Saving our souls and bodies is a continuous process as we abide in Him. Our souls, our minds, our hearts will be renewed as we grow in Him. As our souls are renewed, it will affect our bodies. We will live more Christ-like. We can even experience physical healing, if we continue to believe. It's not easy, I know. I have been waiting a long time but I am not giving up.

Dear Jesus! You have done exceedingly and abundantly above all that we can think or ask. Yet there is no end to what you have done for us by Your sacrifice. We pray that You would continue to increase our faith in You. With You nothing is impossible! To God be the glory Amen! Shalom 2u

1 JOHN 5:18 SINLESS

1Jn 5:18 WEB We know that whoever is born of God doesn't sin, but he who was born of God keeps himself, and the evil one doesn't touch him.

There probably isn't any Born Again believer that doesn't sin. How can JOHN say that one doesn't sin? We must realize that the Born Again believer has 2 identities. The New Man, the New Creation in Christ Jesus and the Old Man, the flesh, the sinful nature. The Bible tells us that the believer's sinful nature, the Old Man died with Jesus and was buried. So we must reckon ourselves dead to sin but alive " in Christ ".

Rom 6:11 KJV Likewise reckon ye also yourselves to be dead indeed unto sin, but alive unto God through Jesus Christ our Lord.

Rom 8:10 KJV And if Christ be in you, the body is dead because of sin; but the Spirit is life because of righteousness.

Dear Jesus! We thank you for living inside us. The more we acknowledge our New Creation in You, the more we will live like You and not sin. Help us to put to death that Old Man and only declare the New Man that we are in You. To God be the glory Amen! Shalom 2u

2 JOHN 1:3 GRACE MERCY PEACE

2Jn 1:3 WEB Grace, mercy, and peace will be with us, from God the Father, and from the Lord Jesus Christ, the Son of the Father, in truth and love.

I get excited every time I read these words. Grace, mercy, shalom/peace is ours by faith not works, through Jesus Christ. When we believe that our "righteousness " is a gift received by faith through Jesus Christ; then we will experience God's grace, mercy, and shalom/peace.

Dear Jesus! We know that in ourselves, we are not righteous. No matter how much we try to keep the Law, we always fail. That's why You came to save us. We rejoice in the work of Your hands, Your sacrifice. You truly are the only way to the Father and receive eternal life. To God be the glory Amen! Shalom 2u

2 JOHN 1:9-11 DOCTRINE OF CHRIST

2Jn 1:9-11 WEB9 Whoever transgresses and doesn't remain in the teaching of Christ, doesn't have God. He who remains in the teaching has both the Father and the Son. 10 If anyone comes to you, and doesn't bring this teaching, don't receive him into your house, and don't welcome him, 11 for he who welcomes him participates in his evil deeds.

One would think that this verse is talking about the law; as in the Ten Commandments. It is not talking about "the Law " as the Ten Commandments but the higher law of loving God with your whole heart and soul; and your neighbor as yourself. When we fulfill the Law of love, we are fulfilling the teaching of Christ. There are many loving people, doing a lot of good works but if they aren't loving God, then they are not following Christ. Verses 10 & 11 tell us to have no part of them.

The only way that we can fulfill the teaching of Christ is by first knowing and believing in Him. This takes time and fellowship with Him.

Dear Jesus! You are the Way, the Truth, and the Life. You also are the Bread of Life. As we abide in You, we are able to love you more and our neighbors as ourselves. We are even able to love those who seem to be unlovable. Just like you, we pray for all and wish that none would perish. To God be the glory Amen! Shalom 2u

Doctrine of Christ: John 3:16-17

Saved by grace not works

Love God & neighbor

John 1:12 KJV But as many as received him, to them gave he power to become the sons of God, even to them that believe on his name:

3 JOHN 1:2 PROSPER

3Jn 1:2 WEB Beloved, I pray that you may prosper in all things and be healthy, even as your soul prospers.

PROSPER : 1. grant a prosperous and expeditious journey, to lead by a direct and easy way 2. to grant a successful issue, to cause to prosper 3. to prosper, be successful

SOUL : the seat of the feelings, desires, affections, aversions (our heart, soul etc.) MIND, WILL,EMOTIONS

There are many that are not sure what God's will is. Here John is telling us as well as in many other places in the Bible; that the will of God is for us to prosper. Jesus began poor so that we may become rich. 2 Corinthians 8:9 WEB For you know the grace of our Lord Jesus Christ, that, though he was rich, yet for your sakes he became poor, that you through his poverty might become rich. Isa 53:5 WEB But he was pierced for our transgressions. He was crushed for our iniquities. The punishment that brought our peace was on him; and by his wounds we are healed.

Our problem is that we have to see it, before we can believe it. God's way is to believe first and then it will come to pass. I'm going through the same fight of faith as you. God says it's His will. I believe that it is His will and all I can do is keep fighting the good fight of faith.

Dear Jesus! We believe in Your great love for us. We believe that You sacrificed all, that we would prosper and be in good health. You waited patiently for us to believe in You. We will wait patiently for Your word not to return void. We praise and thank you now for making us prosperous in all things. To God be the glory Amen! Shalom 2u

3 JOHN 1:3-4 TRUTH

3Jn 1:3-4 WEB 3 For I rejoiced greatly when brothers came and testified about your truth, even as you walk in truth. 4 I have no greater joy than this: to hear about my children walking in truth.

Truth! What is the truth? The truth is that the Gospel is good news. The Truth is that Jesus came to save us because we could not save ourselves. The Truth is that we needed a Savior. Jesus came to save us body, soul, and spirit. His name is Jesus: Joshua saves! Isaiah 53:4☐-☐5 web Surely he has borne our sickness, and carried our suffering; yet we considered him plagued, struck by God, and afflicted. But he was pierced for our transgressions. He was crushed for our iniquities. The punishment that brought our peace was on him; and by his wounds we are healed.

Dear Jesus! You came to save us, redeem us, heal us, to make us whole. There is no life without You. We pray for those who haven't received You yet. In Jesus name, we command the blind to see, the deaf to hear, lame walk, the unclean-clean, the captive: you are set free! To God be the glory Amen! Shalom 2u

JUDE 1:3 CONTEND

Jude 1:3 WEB Beloved, while I was very eager to write to you about our common salvation, I was constrained to write to you exhorting you to contend earnestly for the faith which was once for all delivered to the saints.

Jude is telling us to contend, to fight the good fight of faith. Too often we ask God to do it, instead of using our faith.

1Ti 6:12 KJV Fight the good fight of faith, lay hold on eternal life, whereunto thou art also called, and hast professed a good profession before many witnesses.

2Ti 4:7 KJV I have fought a good fight, I have finished my course, I have kept the faith:

Too often we fight against flesh and blood, instead of the evil spirit behind the person. Ephesians 6:12 WEB

For our wrestling is not against flesh and blood, but against the principalities, against the powers, against the world's rulers of the darkness of this age, and against the spiritual forces of wickedness in the heavenly places.

Dear Jesus! As we abide in You, You give us life given words to defeat the enemy. John 6:63 WEB It is the spirit who gives life. The flesh profits nothing. The words that I speak to you are spirit, and are life. We use Your Spirit filled, live given words now. We come against the spirit of darkness and declare " LIGHT BE ". We come against the spirit of fear and strive and declare Peace/ Shalom in Jesus name Amen! To God be the glory Amen! Shalom 2u

JUDE 1:4 GRACE

Jud 1:4 WEB For there are certain men who crept in secretly, even those who were long ago written about for this condemnation: ungodly men, turning the grace of our God into indecency, and denying our only Master, God, and Lord, Jesus Christ.

Jude is talking about the grace of God. We can go from one extreme to another. I find that grace is largely ignored in the church. It seems to emphasize yourself, doing the right thing. This sounds good but it is not grace but more self righteousness. The other extreme that Jude refers to is that we can do whatever we want because we are under grace. Both are not the true Gospel of Grace.

Dear Jesus! You are the source of all grace. Titus 2:11 WEB For the grace of God has appeared, bringing salvation to all men,

Only by believing and abiding in You can we receive the grace needed to change our souls. When we abide in You, You breathe life, Your grace into our souls. Surely we are saved not by works but by Your grace. To God be the glory Amen! Shalom 2 U

JUDE 1:5 UNBELIEF

Jud 1:5 WEB Now I desire to remind you, though you already know this, that the Lord, having saved the people out of the land of Egypt, afterward destroyed those who didn't believe.

We all are born into the slavery of sin. When we receive Jesus as our Savior, we are set free. It's like the children of Israel being delivered out of bandage in Egypt. They were supposed to continue their journey by faith. Many didn't make it because of unbelief. It is the same today. The Lord saves us. He delivered us but we continued in unbelief. Instead of confessing our New Creation man, we confess who we are in the flesh: the Old Man. Romans 6:6 WEB knowing this, that our old man was crucified with him, that the body of sin might be done away with, so that we would no longer be in bondage to sin.

Dear Jesus! We believe in what You have done for us. The old man was crucified with You and You made us a New Creation in Your image and likeness. We give You praise and thanksgiving for doing such marvelous work in us. We are alive in You. We are righteous in You. In You we have overcome the bondage of sin and live unto righteousness. To God be the glory Amen! Shalom 2 U

JUDE 1:20 PRAYING IN THE SPIRIT

Jud 1:20 WEB But you, beloved, keep building up yourselves on your most holy faith, praying in the Holy Spirit.

There are many interpretations of what it means to pray in the Spirit. Many believe that it is praying to God from our hearts. This sounds good but it doesn't completely agree with what God's word says. The following are several verses that talk about it. To me it is pretty clear that one doesn't know what they are saying at first because they are praying in another unknown language.

Rom 8:26. Likewise the Spirit also helpeth our infirmities: for we know not what we should pray for as we ought: but the Spirit itself maketh intercession for us **with groanings** which cannot be uttered.

Act 2:4 They were all filled with the Holy Spirit, and began to speak with **other languages,** as the Spirit gave them the ability to speak.

1Co 14:4* He who speaks in another language edifies himself, but he who prophesies edifies the church.

Isa 28:11-12 NHEB 11 But he will speak to this nation with stammering lips and a strange language; 12 to whom he said, "This is the resting place. Give rest to weary;" and "This is the refreshing;" but they would not listen.

2Ti 1:6 KJV Wherefore I put thee in remembrance that thou stir up the gift of God, which is in thee by the putting on of my hands.

Dear Jesus! The gift of praying in tongues is very hard for us to understand and believe. The important thing is that we believe in You. It does seem that this gift could help us pray as we should. We ask You now for this gift to be used for Your honor and glory. To God be the glory Amen! Shalom 2u

JUDE 1:21-23 LOVE, BELIEVE, HELP

Jud 1:21-23 EasyEnglish 21 Always remember that God loves you. So you should love and obey him always. And you should love other people. Love like this while you wait for our Lord Jesus Christ to come. He will cause you to live with him always, because he is so very kind. 22 Some people are not completely sure whether God's message is really true. You must be kind to those people and you must try to help them. 23 Some people are turning away from God and they are doing bad things. If they turn away completely, God will punish them in the fire. So you must try to stop those people. Then you will save them, because you will pull them out of the fire. There are other people that you must try to help also. They are like people with very dirty clothes, because of all the bad, dirty things that they do. But you must be very careful, so that they do not lead you away from God. You must be careful like someone who will not even touch those people's dirty clothes.

Jude is first telling us of God's love for us and so we should love others. God wants us to show His love to others because many find it hard to believe. As we share Jesus and His grace to others, we can be used by God to bring them into His Kingdom. Remember it's sharing the Good News that we bring the lost to Jesus.

Dear Jesus! It's only by Your grace and love that we are saved. We pray for the lost. May the blind see,deaf hear,lame walk, unclean be made clean, and the captives set free. 2 Corinthians 13:14 WEBThe grace of the Lord Jesus Christ, God's love, and the fellowship of the Holy Spirit, be with you all. Amen. Shalom 2u

JUDE 1:24-25 GOD IS ABLE

Jud 1:24-25 EasyEnglish 24 God is able to keep you safe so that you do not go the wrong way. He is able to make you completely good and clean inside yourselves. And so he can bring you near to himself. You will come near to the beautiful light that shines from him. You will stand in front of God, who is so very great and good. And you will be very, very happy. 25 He is the only God. He saves us by our Lord Jesus Christ. So everyone should thank him always! Everyone should say how great he is always! He has had all power and authority and he has ruled since time began, until now. And he will have all the power and authority! This is true.

What a beautiful message that Jude is revealing here. It surely is one that has to be believed. It's exceedingly abundantly above all that we can think or ask. God is able to save! There is even a song that sings those words. This is surely Good News. Not only is God able but this is His will and promise to all that believe in Jesus. This is why Jesus came: to save and not condemn. He is able to make us clean inside ourselves. We can not do it on our own.

Dear Jesus! You came to save us and You have all the power to save us. We receive this power, this grace as we abide and trust in You. Believing that we are righteous "in You ". We thank You for giving us Your Divine Power, Your Holy Spirit in us to follow Your commands. To God be the glory Amen! Shalom 2u

REV. 1:5 THE FAITHFUL WITNESS

Rev 1:5 WEB and from Jesus Christ, the faithful witness, the firstborn of the dead, and the ruler of the kings of the earth. To him who loves us, and washed us from our sins by his blood—

All throughout the Old Testament there were prophecies of the coming of a Savior. Jesus was faithful in doing that. He was faithful in proclaiming the Father's love. By His sacrifice, Jesus was faithful to break down the barriers that kept us from being a child of God.

Dear Jesus! You were the firstborn, raised from the dead. We are washed by Your blood and are raised with You. No longer flesh and blood. No longer in bondage to sin. You made us in Your image and likeness. You made us a child of God. To God be the glory Amen! Shalom 2u

REV. 1:6. KINGS & PRIESTS

Rev 1:6 WEB and he made us to be a Kingdom, priests to his God and Father—to him be the glory and the dominion forever and ever. Amen.

We fail most of the time seeing ourselves as Kings and Priests. This is why there is so little power in the church today. We are in Christ Jesus, the King of kings and our great High Priest. Again we need to use our God given authority to rule in the Kingdom of God, to come against the kingdom of darkness. We need to act like Priests and bless one another.

Dear Jesus! You were the faithful witness that took authority over the kingdom of darkness. You are the faithful High Priest that interceded for the lost, the captive, the blind, the deaf and especially for the unclean. And so we pray for those in need. 2 Corinthians 13:14 WEB grace of the Lord Jesus Christ, God's love, and the fellowship of the Holy Spirit, be with you all. Amen. To God be the glory Amen! Shalom 2u

1Pe 2:9. But you are a chosen race, a **royal priesthood**, a holy nation, a people for God's own possession, that you may proclaim the excellence of him who called you out of darkness into his marvelous light:

Rom 5:17 NHEB For if by the trespass of the one, death reigned through the one; so much more will those who receive the abundance of grace and of the gift of righteousness **reign** in life through the one, Jesus Christ.

Luk 10:19 KJV Behold, I give unto you **power** to tread on serpents and scorpions, and over all the power of the enemy: and nothing shall by any means hurt you.

Ecc 8:4 KJV Where the word of a king is, there is power: and who may say unto him, What doest thou?

REV. 1:10 IN THE SPIRIT

Rev 1:10 WEB I was in the Spirit on the Lord's day, and I heard behind me a loud voice, like a trumpet

When you are really "in the Spirit ",you are not having a casual experience. Usually it's when you are alone praising, worshiping, and seeking the Lord. This is the place where you will receive revelation.

Dear Jesus! You always invite us to come to You, to fellowship with you. In Your presence is the fullness of life. In Your presence, You speak to us. You tell us of Your love for us. You encourage us during our trials. You encourage us to walk in love and that with You, we can do all things that You put into our hearts. You give us abundant life. To God be the glory Amen! Shalom 2u

REV 1:16 TWO-EDGED SWORD

Rev 1:16 WEB He had seven stars in his right hand. Out of his mouth proceeded a sharp two-edged sword. His face was like the sun shining at its brightest.

Why does it say " out of His mouth proceeded a two-edged sword " ? When we look at the Armor of God, the last piece is the sword of the Spirit- the word of God. When we are faced with battle, we need to use the sword of the Spirit-God's word. All the other pieces of armor are defensive. The sword of the Spirit is the one that destroys the enemy.

Dear Jesus! You are always victorious in all that you do. Storms, nature, evil men, nothing prevented You from doing the Father's will. Thank you for giving us the armor of God. You have equipped us to be more than conquerors. We shall declare Your Word. Shalom/peace on earth, good will to all in Jesus name. To God be the glory Amen! Shalom 2u

REV 2:2-4 LOVE

Rev 2:2-4 WEB 2 "I know your works, and your toil and perseverance, and that you can't tolerate evil men, and have tested those who call themselves apostles, and they are not, and found them false. 3 You have perseverance and have endured for my name's sake, and have not grown weary. 4 But I have this against you, that you left your first love.

It's saying here that we should judge what people say and do. There were false apostles then as there are today. If you don't know the Word yourself , you can be misled. They were chastised for leaving their first love. Everyone of us is responsible for our relationship with Jesus. You can't rely on the church to do it for you. The church role is to lead you into a personal relationship with Jesus. Then and only then will He truly be the love of your life.

Dear Jesus! We do praise you and thank you for your faithful servants that bring us to You. It's in Your presence that we receive grace and love. Now we can love you more and others as well. To God be the glory Amen! Shalom 2u

Our faith produces work, but work doesn't produce faith. Faith comes from hearing, hearing the word of God. Jesus is the author and finisher of our faith.

REV 2:8-10 BE FAITHFUL

Rev 2:8-10 WEB 8 "To the angel of the assembly in Smyrna write: "The first and the last, who was dead, and has come to life says these things: 9 "I know your works, oppression, and your poverty (but you are rich), and the blasphemy of those who say they are Jews, and they are not, but are a synagogue of Satan. 10 Don't be afraid of the things which you are about to suffer. Behold, the devil is about to throw some of you into prison, that you may be tested; and you will have oppression for ten days. Be faithful to death, and I will give you the crown of life.

We must identify ourselves in Christ. As He was dead and now alive, so are we. We are only poor when we deny Jesus. We are rich when we believe in Him, all that He has done for us and through us. The devil will try to harm us, but it's not God's will. Keep the faith. Fight the battle and receive the crown of life.

Dear Jesus! We are more than conquerors in You. As we look to You during our battles, You give us the faith to win. To God be the glory Amen! Shalom 2u

REV 2:12-14 GOOD & BAD

Rev 2:12-14 WEB 12 "To the angel of the assembly in Pergamum write: "He who has the sharp two-edged sword says these things: 13 "I know your works and where you dwell, where Satan's throne is. You hold firmly to my name, and didn't deny my faith in the days of Antipas my witness, my faithful one, who was killed among you, where Satan dwells. 14 But I have a few things against you, because you have there some who hold the teaching of Balaam, who taught Balak to throw a stumbling block before the children of Israel, to eat things sacrificed to idols, and to commit sexual immorality.

So we see here that the church is receiving good & bad news about their works. First, a good report. They are using the "Two edged sword " to fight against the enemy. The bad report is that they are not calling sin,sin. We see this a lot today. We are called to be against the sin of homosexuality. There are many that think that we are being unkind, unloving. We are called to love the homosexual but come against the sin. God loves everyone; but everyone is called to repent. If anyone doesn't repent and ask Jesus to save them; then they won't be saved.

Dear Jesus! Your Word tells us that all have sin and all need to repent. Thank you for opening our eyes, ears and heart so we would repent. It's Your grace that changes us from going our own way to Your path of righteousness. We pray for those who still need to repent. We command the blind see, deaf hear, lame walk, unclean clean, and the captives free in Jesus name ! Shalom 2u

REV 3:1-4 SLEEPING CHURCH

Rev 3:1-4 WEB 1 "And to the angel of the assembly in Sardis write: "He who has the seven Spirits of God and the seven stars says these things: "I know your works, that you have a reputation of being alive, but you are dead. 2 **Wake up** and keep the things that remain, which you were about to throw away, for I have found no works of yours perfected before my God. 3 Remember therefore how you have received and heard. Keep it and repent. If therefore you won't watch, I will come as a thief, and you won't know what hour I will come upon you. 4 Nevertheless you have a few names in Sardis that didn't defile their garments. They will walk with me in white, for they are worthy.

Unfortunately there are too many churches like this today. They seem to be alive but they're not. They are doing a lot of work but not saving souls. Not declaring the bind to see, the deaf to ear, unclean clean and the captives free. These are the works that we are called to do. Declaring the Good News of God's love and Grace ; using the " sword of the Spirit " will go a long way in doing the works of God.

Dear Jesus! All Your works were good. All were pleasing to the Father. You did all that You were anointed to do: Luke 4:18 WEB "The Spirit of the Lord is on me, because he has anointed me to preach good news to the poor. He has sent me to heal the broken hearted, to proclaim release to the captives, recovering of sight to the blind, to deliver those who are crushed,

You love the sinner but call sin, sin and then you set them free. I know that You are waking us up so that we would be faithful in doing good works. Continue to live in us and work through us we pray. To God be the glory Amen! Shalom 2u

REV 3:7-10 ENDURE & DON'T DENY

Rev 3:7-10 WEB7" To the angel of the assembly in Philadelphia write:"He who is holy, he who is true, he who has the key of David, he who opens and no one can shut, and who shuts and no one opens, says these things: 8"I know your works (behold, I have set before you an open door, which no one can shut), that you have a little power, and kept my word, and didn't deny my name. 9Behold, I give some of the synagogue of Satan, of those who say they are Jews, and they are not, but lie—behold, I will make them to come and worship before your feet, and to know that I have loved you. 10Because you kept my command to endure, I also will keep you from the hour of testing which is to come on the whole world, to test those who dwell on the earth.

Jesus is giving great praise to this church. Even though they were surrounded by satanic forces and had little power; they endured and did not deny His name. How do we deny His name? We claim that He is the Son of God and the Savior of the world. It all seems good and true, but it can be all superficial. When we go through testing and trials, do we endure and not deny His name. Many of us seem to give up too easily. We think that it just might be God's will or that's life. That's not enduring. We need to believe that this testing is not from God but the devil. We need to fight the good fight of faith. In these battles, we need to not deny His name but declare it against all the forces of evil. I believe this is what the church of Philadelphia was doing and it pleased the Lord. During their trials, they declared His name. They declared His Word: the sword of the Spirit.

Dear Jesus! You told us that we would have trials and tribulations, but be of good cheer for You have overcome the world. We declare your name: IN the name of Jesus, we come against the spirit of darkness and declare " LIGHT BE ". We come against fear,doubt, sickness, any force of evil : Shalom/Peace be still in the name of Jesus! Shalom 2u

REV 3:18 BUY WITHOUT MONEY

Rev 3:18 WEBI counsel you to buy from me gold refined by fire, that you may become rich; and white garments, that you may clothe yourself, and that the shame of your nakedness may not be revealed; and eye salve to anoint your eyes, that you may see.

Isa 55:1 KJV Ho, everyone that thirsteth, come ye to the waters, and he that hath no money; come ye, buy, and eat; yea, come, buy wine and milk without money and without price.

We see a mystery here, a riddle. How does one buy from God? How does one buy without money? We see here that God's ways are above our ways and His thoughts higher than ours. It takes "wisdom " to understand God's ways: Proverbs 1:1□-□6 WEBThe proverbs of Solomon, the son of David, king of Israel: to know **wisdom** and instruction; to discern the words of understanding; to receive instruction in wise dealing, in righteousness, justice, and equity; to give prudence to the simple, knowledge and discretion to the young man: that the wise man may hear, and increase in learning; that the man of understanding may attain to sound counsel: to understand a proverb, and parables, the words and riddles of the wise.

God wants the best for us. He wants us to be saved, to be a child of God, eternal life and on and on! So how do we get all that God wants to give us? How do we buy all these good things? It doesn't matter if you're rich or poor. God doesn't want or need our money. God's currency is "FAITH ". Remember: without Faith it is impossible to please God. I know as a father, my children please me the most when they are believing, trusting in me. I'm excited to give them whatever I can. Everything that we want and need, God wants to give it to us and more. Jesus paid the price for it all. It's only by faith in Jesus, can we receive. It starts with asking Jesus to come into your heart and save you. You then receive the free gift of righteousness. From there keep on knowing, believing, and declaring God's promises by faith. It's a battle. The flesh will resist you to believe. But by abiding in Jesus, the source of your faith, you will believe and it will come to pass.

Dear Jesus! Words can not express our thanksgiving for all that you have done for us. We humbly bow down to You. You truly are God's Son and the Savior of the world. To You be all honor and the glory Amen! Shalom 2u

Don't miss out!

Visit the website below and you can sign up to receive emails whenever Shalom Jim publishes a new book. There's no charge and no obligation.

https://books2read.com/r/B-A-LAPW-YKEFC

BOOKS 2 READ

Connecting independent readers to independent writers.

www.ingramcontent.com/pod-product-compliance
Lightning Source LLC
Chambersburg PA
CBHW051243160726
47994CB00003B/1006